EXPLORING CIVIL RIGHTS

THE MOVEMENT

1957

SUSAN TAYLOR

T0002541

Franklin Watts®
An imprint of Scholastic Inc.

Content Consultants

Senator Nan Grogan Orrock
State of Georgia

Crystal R. Sanders, Ph.D.
Associate Professor of History
Pennsylvania State University

Library of Congress Cataloging-in-Publication Data
Names: Taylor, Susan, author.
Title: Exploring civil rights— the movement : 1957 / by Susan Taylor.
Description: First edition. | New York : Franklin Watts, an imprint of Scholastic Inc., [2022] | Series: Exploring civil rights | Includes bibliographical references and index. | Audience: Ages 10–14. | Audience: Grades 5–8.
Identifiers: LCCN 2021020383 (print) | LCCN 2021020384 (ebook) | ISBN 9781338769746 (library binding) | ISBN 9781338769753 (paperback) | ISBN 9781338769760 (ebook)
Subjects: LCSH: African Americans—Civil rights—History—Juvenile literature. | Civil rights movements—United States—History—20th century—Juvenile literature. | Civil rights workers— United States—Juvenile literature. | BISAC: JUVENILE NONFICTION / History / United States / 20th Century | JUVENILE NONFICTION / History / United States / General
Classification: LCC E185.61 .T246 2021 (print) | LCC E185.61 (ebook) | DDC 323.1196/073—dc23
LC record available at https://lccn.loc.gov/2021020383
LC ebook record available at https://lccn.loc.gov/2021020384

10 9 8 7 6 5 4 3 2 1   22 23 24 25 26

Printed in Heshan, China 62
First edition, 2022

ON THE COVER: Elizabeth Eckford arriving for her first day at Central High School in Little Rock, Arkansas.

Series produced by 22MediaWorks, Inc.
President LARY ROSENBLATT
Book design by FABIA WARGIN and AMELIA LEON
Editor SUSAN ELKIN
Copy Editor LAURIE LIEB
Fact Checker BRETTE SEMBER
Photo Researcher DAVID PAUL PRODUCTIONS

PREVIOUS PAGE: Troops from the U.S. Army's 101st Airborne Division were ordered to Arkansas to escort and protect the Little Rock Nine at Central High School.

Prayer Pilgrimage for Freedom, page 24

Table of Contents

Daisy Bates, page 46

A class of Black students squeeze into the pews of a Baptist church to create a one-room schoolhouse in 1949.

The Way It Was

In December 1865, the Thirteenth Amendment to the U.S. Constitution abolished slavery in the United States. By the early 1870s, former slaveholding states in the South created Black codes to strictly limit the freedom of their Black citizens. These restrictions were known as "**Jim Crow**" laws, and they controlled where people who used to be enslaved could live and work.

Jim Crow laws were expanded in the 1880s to keep Black citizens from voting or receiving a proper education. In many parts of the South, they were forced to use separate restaurants, schools, restrooms, parks, and other public places. This practice is known as **segregation**. Although laws said that these spaces should be "separate but equal," facilities for Black people were almost always inferior to those assigned to white citizens.

It was not uncommon for Black citizens in the South to be kidnapped and beaten, shot, or killed for small violations of Jim Crow laws. **Lynchings** and white mob violence frequently terrorized many Black communities. Black churches were burned down, and Black homes attacked. **Discrimination** against Black Americans also existed in the North and elsewhere in the nation, but less so than in the South at the time.

Fighting Back

Segregation, Jim Crow laws, and discrimination denied Black Americans the same **civil rights** as white Americans. In the face of **oppression** and terror, some Black Americans organized to fight inequality. The first civil rights organization in the United States was founded in 1896 as the National Association of Colored Women's Clubs. In 1909, an interracial group of **activists** formed the National Association for the Advancement of Colored People (NAACP). The NAACP called for an end to segregation in schools, public transportation, and other areas of daily life. The group also focused on making the American public aware of the violence against Black people.

In the following years, new civil rights groups emerged. Christian ministers, African American lawyers, and Black youth were especially important in organizing and supporting the emerging civil rights movement. The decade between 1955 and 1965 would serve as the heart of the movement, as action and long-awaited progress began to take shape.

1957

This book takes a look at the most important events in the struggle for equality during the year 1957. In January, civil rights leaders gathered in Atlanta, Georgia, to form a national organization with the Reverend Dr. Martin Luther King, Jr., at its head, bringing him national recognition. In May, at the Prayer Pilgrimage for Freedom in Washington, DC, King told the crowd that there could be no freedom for Black people without safe access to the voting booth. In September, Congress passed the Civil Rights Act of 1957 and nine Black students **integrated** Central High School in Little Rock, Arkansas. Backlash from these events would inspire and motivate Black and white youth around the country to act in the greatest social justice campaign of the last century. ∎

The Reverend Ralph Abernathy (right) and his assistant inspect the damage to Abernathy's house after it was bombed.

1

Leaders Organize for Change

Following the momentum gained by the success of the 1955–1956 Montgomery bus **boycott**, civil rights leaders gathered to create a unified front in 1957. The NAACP continued to push civil rights issues on a national level, but many activists had been acting independently against injustice. Leaders like Dr. Martin Luther King, Jr., recognized the importance of creating one organization that could bring their issues forward as a larger unit.

Activist groups gathered at Ebenezer Baptist Church in Atlanta on January 10 and 11, 1957. They formed a regional organization to coordinate protests across the South. Sixty leaders from 10 states voted to form a permanent organization called the Southern Negro Leaders Conference on Transportation and Nonviolent Integration (also known as the Southern Leaders Conference).

The two-day meeting focused on the goal of creating significant change for Black Americans, particularly in the South. The new organization's leaders sent **telegrams** to President Dwight D. Eisenhower and Vice President Richard M. Nixon. They created an outline explaining their positions on oppression in the South.

Desegregation of city buses was the first issue that the Montgomery Improvement Association addressed.

Throughout the civil rights movement, Black churches were one of the most common targets of bombings and threats.

Violence Follows

The gathering of Black leaders in Atlanta called attention to key figures in the movement. Those who opposed integration and equal rights for Black Americans stepped up violent attacks on many of them. Ralph Abernathy was King's closest friend and adviser, a minister from Montgomery, Alabama. On January 10, the same day as the Atlanta gathering, Abernathy's home and four Black churches in Montgomery were bombed. No one was injured, but the bombing caused a lot of damage. Abernathy was safe in Atlanta, and the bombings only strengthened his commitment to the movement.

Only the Beginning

The initial meeting among civil rights leaders established the beginning of what would become a strong alliance of individuals committed to change for Black Americans. On February 14, a second meeting was held in New Orleans, Louisiana, with King and 96 other Black religious leaders. Here they established a board of directors and elected officers, including King as their new president and Abernathy as treasurer.

Dr. King reads a telegram to President Eisenhower, urging him to speak out against segregation.

Activist Bayard Rustin (right) worked with King and Abernathy (left).

Financial support for the new organization was hard to come by. King had not yet become a national icon for civil rights, and some people were concerned the group would cause trouble. Many Black southerners feared **retribution** for being associated with the new organization. ■

The Dred Scott Decision of 1857

Fewer than 100 years before the civil rights movement began, slavery was still commonly practiced throughout the South. One important Supreme Court case, known as the Dred Scott decision, gave momentum to the antislavery movement and led America closer to civil war.

Dred Scott was born into slavery in 1799 in the state of Virginia. After his first owner died, he moved with his new owner, Dr. John Emerson, to Missouri, a state where slavery was also legal. In 1832, Emerson moved to Illinois and later Wisconsin, taking Scott along with him. Both those states, however, had outlawed slavery. After Emerson died, his wife, Irene, returned with Scott to Missouri. Scott filed lawsuits for his freedom and freedom for his wife and children. Although it was a slave state, Missouri law at that time stated that once an enslaved person entered a free state, they became free, and remained that way when they returned to a state where slavery was still legal.

Backed by their church and **abolitionists**, Dred Scott's case reached the U.S. Supreme Court. On March 6, 1857, the court ruled against Scott in the now infamous Dred Scott decision. Scott lost his fight for freedom. The Supreme Court decision outraged abolitionists, widening the divide between the northern and southern states and eventually contributing to the Civil War.

Despite losing his case, Scott was actually freed soon after the Supreme Court decision. He died one year later.

Dr. King was only 28 years old when he became known around the world.

2

Dr. King on the World Stage

The newly formed Southern Leaders Conference believed that there would be little progress for Black Americans if the government did not enforce the 1954 Supreme Court decision *Brown v. Board of Education,* which ordered states to integrate their public schools. Its members and other activists understood that the decision affected other areas of public life. They wanted to show that "separate but equal" was no longer acceptable. Equal rights for Black Americans should extend to buses, public facilities, and especially voting booths.

At the February meeting, leaders sent a telegram to President Eisenhower asking him to publicly support integration in schools and the now three-year-old *Brown* decision.

President Eisenhower would not publicly support enforcement of school integration because he did not want to lose the approval of those in Congress who were against it.

When Eisenhower declined to do so, Dr. King and his colleagues wrote that they would bring protesters to "the capitol in order to call the nation's attention to the violence and organized terror directed toward [men], women, and children who merely seek freedom."

To accomplish this task and publicize these important issues, King and others decided to organize a prayer pilgrimage to Washington, DC. As plans for the pilgrimage were being made, King's profile as head of the movement gained international attention.

A Visit Abroad

In early March 1957, as the movement and King's leadership became more widely known, he and his wife, Coretta Scott King, traveled to the African country of Ghana to celebrate its independence from British rule. King's church congregation and the Montgomery Improvement Association, the organization of which King was president and which staged the bus boycott the previous year, gathered funds to send the couple to Africa.

Dr. Martin Luther King, Jr., and wife, Coretta, at the Ghanaian independence ceremony.

Black Americans felt a connection to the freedom won by this Black African country and to the joy Ghanaians felt as they exercised their rights as citizens of their own country for the first time. Formerly known as the Gold Coast, the new country of Ghana was led by Prime Minister Kwame Nkrumah. To celebrate the occasion, Nkrumah invited political leaders from all over the globe.

King was recognized as one of those leaders, attending the celebration alongside other American activists and politicians.

On March 6, 1957, the celebration marking Ghana's independence began. King recalled seeing nearly half a million people gather for the event. It moved him to tears. King's lessons from Ghana would inspire him to lead action back in the United States.

Prime Minister Kwame Nkrumah is carried on the shoulders of citizens celebrating independence.

The flag of Ghana

Ghana's Fight for Freedom

Until the 1950s, territories in Africa were occupied by European countries, and those ruling governments controlled much of the continent's wealth. Under British rule, Ghana prospered and its citizens had more formal education, but the Ghanaian people had little political power.

Beginning in the 1940s, residents of the Gold Coast, led by Kwame Nkrumah, started to organize against British rule. His group rallied workers and farmers to strike. They wrote a constitution and organized an election. In 1956, Nkrumah's group proposed independence from Britain, and the British government agreed to set March 6, 1957, as the day for independence.

King Meets Nixon

Another important outcome of King's visit to Ghana was meeting Vice President Richard Nixon, who was also there. King invited Nixon to visit the South, where the struggles of Black people in Alabama were similar to those of the citizens of the Gold Coast. Although Nixon didn't accept King's offer to visit, he invited King to a meeting in Washington, DC, when they returned, marking national recognition of King's role in the civil rights movement. ■

More than 1,000 Africans welcomed Vice President Richard Nixon on his arrival in Ghana.

The view from the Lincoln Memorial at the Prayer Pilgrimage for Freedom.

3

Prayer Pilgrimage for Freedom

A pilgrimage is a journey to a sacred place. For Americans looking for freedom, traveling to the nation's capital where laws for the country are made was such a journey. Dr. King returned from Ghana determined to take the movement to the politicians in Washington, DC. The Prayer Pilgrimage for Freedom was designed as a march through the nation's capital that would end at the steps of the Lincoln Memorial.

Not all civil rights leaders, however, thought the pilgrimage was a good idea. During a planning meeting in April 1957, some leaders thought it might backfire to confront the president at his doorstep and embarrass him. When King pressed forward with his idea, his colleagues framed the event as a day of prayer commemorating the third anniversary of the 1954 Supreme Court decision *Brown v. Board of Education*, which outlawed segregation in public schools.

On May 17, 1957, nearly 25,000 Black and white Americans gathered on the steps of the Lincoln Memorial in Washington. It was, at the time, the largest civil rights demonstration ever. Although less than half of its intended participants showed up, the event featured three hours of prayer, songs, and speeches aimed at bringing attention to the civil rights movement. Singers, leaders, and ministers took to the stage to inspire the crowd.

King greets demonstrators in the crowd who share the goal of eliminating segregation in schools.

In the Woman **Suffrage** Procession, Black suffragist Ida B. Wells refused to march in the back. She joined the group from Illinois, where she marched between white supporters.

History Inspires

The Prayer Pilgrimage was not the first large-scale protest to demand voting rights in the nation's capital. In 1913, the Woman Suffrage Procession was the first parade for social justice in Washington, DC. On the day before President Woodrow Wilson's inauguration, between 5,000 and 10,000 women marched with floats and bands, all demanding the right to vote. Some Black women joined the march, but, as in other places in society, were segregated to the back of the parade. Despite the efforts of the protesters, it took until 1920 for women to win their right to vote.

Leaders Speak Up

Of the many civil rights leaders in attendance, prominent names like Rosa Parks, Harry Belafonte, Mahalia Jackson, and Mordecai Johnson helped inspire the crowd. By this time, Rosa Parks was widely known, having sparked the Montgomery bus boycott two years earlier. Belafonte was a Jamaican American singer who over time helped King organize demonstrations and raise money for the movement.

Gospel singer Mahalia Jackson performed for the crowd. Mordecai Johnson was the first African American president of Howard University.

Roy Wilkins, leader of the NAACP, also addressed the crowd. Many of these speakers had experienced prejudice throughout their lives and strongly supported the campaign.

The most powerful moment of the demonstration came when King addressed the crowd. As the final speaker of the three-hour event, King urged President Eisenhower and members of Congress to take action. He asked them to protect voting rights for African Americans. His speech, now famously called "Give Us the Ballot," addressed the inequalities and lack of access faced by many Black voters.

Although the Prayer Pilgrimage was organized as a response to segregated education, King believed voting rights were a fundamental piece of civil rights, and if more Black people were voting, they could create change in other areas.

Black and white Americans from 30 different states traveled to Washington, DC, for the Prayer Pilgrimage for Freedom.

Mahalia Jackson sold 22 million records and performed in concert halls around the world.

Singer Turns Activist

In her biography, Mahalia Jackson describes the challenges she found trying to buy a house in Chicago, Illinois. Whenever she looked at a house in a mostly white neighborhood, she was told by real estate agents or owners that the house wasn't available to her. Eventually, after finding a house to buy, she received threats from white neighbors and feared for her safety. Because of these experiences Jackson was an outspoken advocate for civil rights.

Later, journalists remarked on the power of King's speech to appeal to the audience and address the issues. Two days later, King gave a sermon at Philadelphia's Zion Baptist Church. More than 1,800 people crammed into the church, and hundreds more gathered outside, to hear the powerful voice of the popular new leader.

After the success of the Prayer Pilgrimage, King traveled throughout the United States preaching his message about the urgency and **righteousness** of equality for Black Americans. In 1957 alone, King traveled 780,000 miles and made 208 speeches.

After the Prayer Pilgrimage, King drew supporters of all races to his speaking engagements across the nation.

King's meeting with Vice President Nixon demanded more change from the leaders in Washington.

A White House Meeting

Civil rights tensions remained high in the South, and leaders in Washington, DC, did not know how to approach the unrest. On June 13, 1957, Nixon held the promised meeting with King and Ralph Abernathy at the White House, showing the nation that the vice president acknowledged the voices of the protesters. It was an important step for King and other civil rights leaders. Support from political leaders was crucial for success in the South. King hoped to convince those people in power to pass laws that would protect Black citizens.

During the two-hour meeting with the vice president, King and Abernathy discussed nine items that they had agreed on ahead of time as most critical. These included the right to vote, the importance of passing a new law guaranteeing civil rights, and the urging of the political leaders to visit the South and validate the struggles of the movement. The meeting inspired Nixon to work with Congress to pass civil rights legislation just a few months later.

The following year, King and other Black leaders finally met with President Eisenhower in the White House to discuss race relations in the South.

King (left) and other civil rights leaders meet with President Eisenhower (third from left) at the White House in June 1958.

The SCLC

In August 1957, at its third meeting in Montgomery, the Southern Negro Leaders Conference on Transportation and Nonviolent Integration voted to change its name permanently to the Southern Christian Leadership Conference (SCLC). The name change reflected how the organization mobilized church congregations to promote important issues, like desegregation and voting rights. Many of its leaders were also Christian ministers. The organization established its office in Atlanta and hired one staff member to help organize protests. Its first major campaign, the Crusade for Citizenship, would begin with the goal of registering and educating new Black voters.

Both Atlanta and Montgomery became central locations and battlegrounds for the growing civil rights movement, thanks to SCLC leaders. Most importantly, the three meetings in 1957 helped establish a central organization that would confront important civil rights issues for the next decade. ■

A Family of Activists

King's children carried on the tradition of civil rights activism. His son Martin Luther King III headed the organization between 1997 and 2003. His daughter Bernice King was elected to lead the organization in 2009 but declined the position to focus on the organization founded by her mother, Coretta Scott King. She is currently president of The King Center in Atlanta.

Bernice King continues her father's work as a minister and activist.

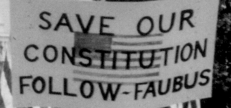

SAVE OUR
CONSTITUTION
FOLLOW-FAUBUS

White residents of
Little Rock, Arkansas, march
in support of Governor Faubus's
decision to block school
integration.

4

The Little Rock Nine

In 1955, one year after *Brown v. Board of Education*, a second Supreme Court decision, known as *Brown II*, ordered school districts to integrate with "all deliberate speed." However, that decision had also been ignored by leadership in the South. In the spring and summer of 1957, the NAACP embarked on a campaign to enforce integration in the public schools of the South. Arkansas seemed a relatively safe choice to initiate this campaign. The path to integration seemed easier there than in other southern states. The University of Arkansas School of Law had integrated in 1948 and the Little Rock Public Library did so in 1951. By 1957, seven out of Arkansas's eight state universities were integrated and the public bus system desegregated.

Orval Faubus gained national attention as an opponent of integration.

In fact, some schools in Arkansas, including Fayetteville and Charleston public schools, had already quietly desegregated as early as 1954.

Even so, forced desegregation was a controversial subject in Arkansas's capital city of Little Rock. Governor Orval Faubus was under pressure from an angry white public who strongly opposed school integration. Because of this pressure, the governor did not make the transition an easy one.

A Plan to Integrate

The superintendent of Little Rock schools, Virgil Blossom, worked to comply with the *Brown v. Board of Education* and *Brown II* rulings. He planned that high schools in the city would be the first to integrate, beginning in September 1957. At Little Rock Central High School, all 1,900 students were white. In that district, there were 517 Black students who attended all-Black schools. Eighty of them initially volunteered to attend the all-white school, but the school board approved the addition of only 17 Black students.

As superintendent, Virgil Blossom saw his plan to integrate Little Rock's schools face strong opposition from white parents in the district.

CAPACITY 100
37 CLASSROOMS - COMPL

DATE OF CONTRACT APRI
DATE OF OCCUPANCY ESTIMATED, SE
COST OF SITE $86,650.00
COST OF BUILDING, INCLUDING FEES $949,989.00 (ESTIMATE)
SQUARE FOOT COST $ 9.87
NITURE NT NO ESTIMATE
S AND ENT NO ESTIMATE
NOT AVAILABLE

During the summer, Daisy Gaston Bates, president of the Arkansas NAACP, carefully selected 17 young men and women who she felt would be strong enough to deal with the expected hostility of parents, students, and even some teachers. The chosen students were counseled before the start of school to help them manage their fear and behavior in the face of the public's anger. Eight of those selected later chose to stay at their all-Black schools instead. The final nine students became known as the Little Rock Nine.

The Little Rock Nine and Daisy Bates: bottom row, left to right: Thelma Mothershed, Minnijean Brown, Elizabeth Eckford, Gloria Ray; top row, left to right: Jefferson Thomas, Melba Patillo, Terrence Roberts, Carlotta Walls, Daisy Bates, Ernest Green

Minnijean Brown joins her white schoolmates practicing a school cheer as members of the 101st Airborne Division stand by for protection.

A Student Remembers

Minnijean Brown recalled her role in desegregating Little Rock many years later. She remembered that the students who chose to transfer to the all-white school weren't necessarily looking to be a part of history. The white school was actually closer to her home and more convenient. But she remembers feeling excited: "Wow! I can meet some other kids." On September 4, 1957, she wasn't thinking of Supreme Court rulings or civil rights—she was planning what to wear for her first day at a new high school.

Hostility Greets the Students

On September 2, 1957, just two days before the first day of school, Governor Faubus ordered the Arkansas National Guard to be prepared to prevent the Little Rock Nine from entering Central High School. The governor claimed he was acting for the students' own safety and protection. In a televised address, he insisted that integration would cause violence, citing an increase in gun sales, among other factors. This response from the governor

Crowds watch the crisis unfold at the steps of Little Rock's Central High School.

Angry white citizens follow student Elizabeth Eckford as she unsuccessfully attempts to attend her first day of school.

clearly defied **federal** law. However, a judge ruled that desegregation would occur as planned.

On the first day of school, September 4, 1957, Daisy Bates arranged for the nine Black students to carpool to school. But one of the nine, Elizabeth Eckford, wasn't aware of the plan. Her family didn't have a telephone and Bates was unable to reach her. Eckford arrived at school first, and alone.

She was greeted by the Arkansas National Guard, who stopped her from entering. An angry crowd of about 400 white people threatened her with violence and spat on her.

As the other Black students arrived, guardsmen told them that the school was "out of bounds" to them. The students were forced to return home and await further direction.

Journalists and spectators watch as four of the nine Black students are turned away from entering Little Rock Central High School.

Daisy Bates was sometimes the target of intimidation due to her role in organizing the Little Rock Nine.

The Legacy of Daisy Bates

In July 2020, the governor of Arkansas and mayor of Little Rock announced a plan to honor the work of Daisy Bates and her fight for school integregation by placing her statue in the U.S. Capitol building. Each state places statues in the National Statuary Hall in Washington, DC, to honor their citizens who have made important contri-butions to society. Bates will join other civil rights leaders displayed in the Capitol building, including Rosa Parks and Martin Luther King, Jr.

The images in the media from September 4 brought national attention to the **plight** of the Little Rock Nine. Although they missed their first day at a new school, the fight wasn't over. It was the first time the *Brown v. Board of Education* decision had been tested. By ignoring federal law, Governor Faubus had misused state authority. President Eisenhower faced a difficult situation. In order to uphold the Constitution, he would be forced to engage in a battle in Arkansas. ■

Governor Faubus sought President Eisenhower's help in delaying integration of Arkansas schools.

Thurgood Marshall arrives at the court where he will argue against the decisions of Arkansas governor Orval Faubus.

5

Full Steam Ahead

For three weeks, the Little Rock Nine were in limbo, unsure of their status at their new school. They formed a study group while they waited for guidance from officials. NAACP leader Daisy Bates continued to help the students prepare for the year ahead while politicians discussed the problem at hand.

After the first confrontation in front of Little Rock Central High School, attorneys from the U.S. Department of Justice requested an **injunction** against the use of the troops. President Eisenhower then appealed to Governor Faubus directly. On September 14, during the president's vacation in Rhode Island, he invited Faubus to meet with him. Eisenhower wasn't particularly supportive of the 1954 *Brown* decision, but he knew the importance of following the Constitution. Faubus agreed with Eisenhower

Prohibited from entering Central High School, the Little Rock Nine form a study group.

to respect the decisions of the Supreme Court and proceed with integration by removing the Arkansas National Guard.

However, upon returning to Arkansas, Faubus did not immediately remove the troops preventing the Little Rock Nine from attending school. On September 20, federal judge Ronald Davies ordered Faubus to abide by the *Brown* decision. Judge Davies ruled that the guardsmen must be removed and the students allowed to enter the school. Governor Faubus had no choice now but to obey.

State v. Federal

The disagreement between the governor of Arkansas and the federal government was an issue that affected many of the southern states. Many governors and state legislators believed they had the right to govern their residents using their own set of laws. They viewed the enforcement of federal policies, such as integration, as an abuse of power. But in the end, the decisions made by the president, the Supreme Court, and Congress overruled state laws.

After removing the Arkansas National Guard, Governor Faubus stationed local police at the school, armed with riot guns and tear gas. Faubus claimed it was for the students' protection.

White and Black youth face off in front of Central High School.

On September 23, the nine Black students returned to school. This time they were greeted by an even bigger crowd of nearly 1,000 white protesters. The students managed to access the school through a side door, but by then the unruly crowd had become a rioting mob.

Black journalists covering the event were attacked. Once again, the police removed the students from the school for their own safety. The second attempt to integrate had failed. On September 23, President Eisenhower signed an **executive order** directing Faubus to follow through on Judge Davies's orders to integrate Central High school. The following day, the mayor of Little Rock, Woodrow Mann, appealed to President Eisenhower for help.

An angry mob of white people shoves a newspaper reporter in Little Rock as tensions run high.

LITTLE ROCK CENTR

The Little Rock Nine receive protection by federal troops for their first day of school.

In a telegram, Mann told the president, "the situation is out of control and police cannot disperse the mob."

One thousand troops from the U.S. Army's 101st Airborne Division were sent to Little Rock to maintain order. It was the first time federal troops had been mobilized against southerners since the Civil War.

With soldiers protecting them, the teenage students finally attended their first day of school on September 25, 1957. Escorted by the federal troops as army helicopters circled overhead, the Little Rock Nine walked through the front doors of Central High at 9:22 a.m. Protesters outside, chanting "two-four-six-eight, we ain't gonna integrate," continued to

A fight scene from *West Side Story*.

West Side Story

The musical *West Side Story* debuted on Broadway on September 26, 1957. The play takes place in a multiracial neighborhood in New York City in the 1950s. Two rival gangs, one made up of U.S. citizens from Puerto Rico and the other a group of white teens, fight for control of their neighborhood. The plot explores the effects of poverty and racism, and the struggle of people of color in America.

The show featured a racially diverse cast of actors. Most importantly, the musical embraced multiculturalism and reinforced the importance of tolerance.

clash with the soldiers. Nearly 750 white high school students were absent because parents refused to send their children to Central High that day.

On September 26, Governor Faubus went on television and criticized the actions of President Eisenhower. However, the law prevailed.

The Fight Continues

During the next few months, the number of federal troops remaining at Little Rock's Central High School dwindled as fewer and fewer protesters swarmed the entryway. A small number of troops remained to patrol the school halls to prevent violence throughout the school year. Two guards were assigned to each Black student for their protection, but trouble still followed.

The Little Rock Nine were driven to school with a federal troop escort until October 25th, when conditions had finally calmed enough for them to arrive at school on their own.

Many white students were cruel to their new Black classmates. The Little Rock Nine were taunted and assaulted, sometimes spat on by their classmates. One boy hung a straw **effigy**, or figurine representing a Black person, from a tree. The lockers of the Black students were trashed. Racist students pushed, choked, and pelted members of the Little Rock Nine with rocks.

Acid was thrown in Melba Patillo's face, and raw eggs poured on her head. Gloria Ray was pushed down a flight of stairs. None of the nine shared classes, and claims of mistreatment were difficult to prove. The school did little to help the Black students.

Assaults followed the students home as well. Phone calls with threats were common, and many people feared for the safety of the nine. Gloria Ray's mother was fired from her job with the State of Arkansas for refusing to remove her daughter from the school.

Melba Patillo experienced feelings of isolation throughout the school year.

Minnijean Brown (second from left) with her mother (far left), and members of the family she lived with while attending school in New York City.

Moving Up and Out

In early 1958, Minnijean Brown was suspended, and later **expelled**, for an incident at school. She had dropped a bowl of chili that splattered on two boys who were **harassing** and bullying her. Brown would be the only one of the Little Rock Nine who would not make it to the end of the school year. After she left Central High School, she moved to New York, where she finished her education.

As the only senior in the group, Ernest Green became the first Black graduate of the school. A former Boy Scout, Green was an active member of the community and regularly attended church. Martin Luther King, Jr., attended his graduation on May 27, 1958, marking the significance of the occasion.

The remaining seven of the original Little Rock Nine students would not return to Central High the following year. In fact, none of the Central High School students would have that opportunity.

Ernest Green proudly represents the Little Rock Nine on graduation day.

Black Athletes Win Big

While the United States attempted to integrate its schools, Black athletes were breaking barriers on the international stage. Althea Gibson was a Black tennis player who quickly rose to the top of her game, winning titles at Wimbledon and the U.S. Open. Later that year, the Associated Press voted Gibson the Female Athlete of the Year, the first Black American to receive the honor.

Charlie Sifford was a Black golfer who often endured racial abuse and threats. In 1957, Sifford won the Long Beach Open, the first Black man to win a major golf championship. Later, he became the first Black man to play on the PGA Tour and the first Black golfer inducted into the World Golf Hall of Fame.

The Lost Year

The events of 1957 in Little Rock affected Arkansas schoolchildren for the next several years as lawyers and politicians continued to fight integration. In September 1958, citizens of Little Rock voted overwhelmingly against integration and for closing the schools. That month, Governor Faubus enacted a newly passed state law that allowed schools to close instead of desegregating. In response, all of Little Rock's public high schools closed for the 1958–1959 school year. City leaders chose to keep 3,665 Black and white students from receiving an education instead of integrating the schools.

Some African American students were educated at home during the year that Little Rock schools were closed.

Van Buren High School, also located in Little Rock, successfully integrated in 1957 but without the national attention given to Central High School.

Many families were forced to leave the state to look for education for their children. Other kids traveled by bus daily to schools in other cities or moved in with relatives in other parts of the state. White students had more options, with over 44 percent enrolling in private schools. Many Black students did no academic work that year. Some found jobs or joined the military, and many of them never returned to finish their education.

President Clinton presents the Congressional Gold Medal to the Little Rock Nine on November 9, 1999.

Congressional Gold Medal

In 1999, President Bill Clinton recognized the Little Rock Nine for their role in the civil rights movement by awarding them the Congressional Gold Medal. This medal, which signals the nation's appreciation of people's achievement and impact on history or culture, is one of the two highest **civilian** honors. First awarded to George Washington in 1776, the Congressional Gold Medal has been awarded to just under 200 people throughout the country's history.

A Hard-Fought Happy Ending

Seven of the remaining Little Rock Nine finished their education at other schools across the country. Elizabeth Eckford joined the army and later became a social studies teacher. Melba Patillo moved to California and became a journalist and writer. Ernest Green worked on Wall Street. Minnijean Brown became an activist and worked for the U.S. Department of the Interior.

Little Rock's high schools reopened in August 1959 after a federal court overruled the governor's school closure. Throughout the South in the years following, the same kind of violent resistance to integration would continue to play out in many areas of public life. ∎

Six of the Little Rock Nine outside the Supreme Court of the United States in 1958.

An election official consults a book of registered voters at a polling location.

6

The Civil Rights Act of 1957

Civil liberties, such as freedom of speech and freedom of religion, are protected by the U.S. Constitution. This means that every person is entitled to these basic rights and that police officers, lawyers, and politicians cannot **infringe** on these rights. The Fourteenth Amendment, Fifteenth Amendment, and the Civil Rights Act of 1875 were all passed just after the Civil War. The Fourteenth Amendment to the Constitution gave African Americans equal rights under the law. This meant that all citizens, not just white men, had freedom of speech, freedom of religion, and other fundamental rights, regardless of their skin color.

In 1870, the Fifteenth Amendment gave all male citizens, regardless of race, the right to vote.

Women were still denied the vote for another 50 years, but Black men could finally make their voices heard.

The Civil Rights Act of 1875 enforced the idea of "equality of all men before the law," which outlawed racial discrimination in public places. Unfortunately, in 1883 the Supreme Court **nullified** the civil rights bill, making it no longer effective. That was the last time the government passed a law to protect the rights of all citizens, regardless of color, until the 1960s.

African American men faced obstacles to voting, even after they gained the right in 1870.

ORIGINAL

POLL TAX RECEIPT
STATE OF TEXAS
COUNTY OF BEXAR

PRECINCT // PAGE_____ LINE_____

San Antonio, Texas, _____ 193__

No 845073

1931

RECEIVED OF Mrs. Carrie Turk.

the sum of One and 50/100 Dollars in payment of Poll Tax for the year 1931

ADDRESS 2154 Feris City Rd

AGE	LENGTH OF RESIDENCE			Native Born } Citizen of United States and
	State	County	City	Naturalized } was born in Kans.
40	20	20	20	Occupation Hwf. Where Issued off

Race - White - Colored   Sex - Male - Female

The said Tax Payer being duly sworn by me says that the above is correct. All of which I Certify.

By E. F. Moss Deputy.

Maury Maverick
Tax Collector, Bexar County, Texas.

A receipt for a poll tax in San Antonio, Texas, shows payment for voting in 1931.

Barriers at the Polls

Dr. King, the SCLC, and the NAACP understood that protests and Supreme Court cases pushed civil rights forward, but only laws passed by Congress could fully protect the rights of Black Americans. They appealed to the president to pass a law that would protect Black voting rights.

In the South, Black voters found it hard to make their vote count, due to several discriminatory factors. One of the most challenging hurdles was the **poll tax**. Some states, especially in the South, attached a fee to the ability to vote. This meant that to register to vote, a citizen must have enough money to pay for it. Many poor Black Americans could not afford the required fee.

CHANCERY COURT

COUNTY

COUNTY

Black Americans and white Americans stand in segregated lines as they wait to register to vote in Fayette County, Georgia.

Similarly, some states required a **literacy** test, meaning those who couldn't read or write would not be able to vote. Without the same access to education that white citizens had, many Black Americans could not pass the literacy test.

Safety for Black Americans at registration and polling places was also a primary goal of the civil rights movement. Black citizens were threatened, scared away by police dogs, or feared losing their jobs if they tried to vote. In Mississippi, a local minister named George Lee was shot and killed for registering Black voters in the mid-1950s. Many Black Americans were justifiably frightened to cast their ballots.

A group of women exercise their right to vote at a polling station in Pennsylvania.

Voter registration drives and literacy classes were held in church basements as participation in elections among African Americans increased.

Civil rights leaders worked hard to register voters across the South by driving voters to polls, holding literacy classes, and encouraging Black candidates to run for election. But these efforts needed to be supported by federal laws protecting Black people's rights as citizens.

A Reluctant Congress

U.S. Attorney General Herbert Brownell proposed a new civil rights bill in 1957, this time protecting voting rights for Black Americans and enforcing school integration. But civil rights at this time were still controversial in Congress. Many legislators, especially from the South, did not want to support the bill because they were opposed to integration. Some believed the federal government should not interfere. To pass, the bill would need approval from both Republicans and Democrats in the Senate before it could be signed into law by President Eisenhower.

U.S. Attorney General Herbert Brownell was a strong supporter of integration and encouraged politicians to support the civil rights bill of 1957.

Black voters and white voters stand in line at a polling station in Tallahassee, Florida.

Senate Majority Leader Lyndon B. Johnson from Texas knew that he would need to make changes to the bill in order to get it passed. Eventually, the language in the bill looked very little like the original version. Notably, it no longer included provisions about school integration. That topic was eliminated from the bill altogether.

The remaining goal of the bill was still intact—to increase the number of registered Black voters. But the bill was modified so that a person who interfered with voter registration, or used intimidation against

Black citizens to prevent them from reaching the polls, would not suffer significant consequences.

Many activists saw the revised civil rights bill as shallow, offering little protection for Black voters. But others saw it as an important step because it symbolized progress. The U.S. government recognized that the basic rights of all its citizens, especially Black Americans, were not protected by existing law. The proposed bill, while not perfect, would at least be an improvement. It also meant the voices of King and other civil rights leaders and activists were being heard.

Senator Lyndon Johnson (middle) discusses the civil rights bill with colleagues. Johnson would later become president.

Strom Thurmond (right) and his wife leaving the Senate chamber after his filibuster.

A Filibuster Makes History

The revised civil rights bill passed easily in the House of Representatives with support from both parties. But in the Senate, it was met with more resistance. Senator Strom Thurmond from South Carolina was strongly opposed to the bill even after changes were made. He tried to keep the bill from passing by holding the longest **filibuster** in history. For 24 hours and 18 minutes, Thurmond stalled the Senate meeting in an attempt to keep the bill from becoming a law.

Thurmond stood before his colleagues and read from the Declaration of Independence, the Bill of Rights, George Washington's Farewell Address, and other texts in order to stall a vote. As night came, cots from a nearby hotel were brought in for the other senators to sleep on while Thurmond talked.

Despite Thurmond's efforts, the vote was held and the bill passed. President Eisenhower signed the Civil Rights Act of 1957 into law on September 9.

President Eisenhower signs the Civil Rights Act of 1957.

In addition to addressing voting issues, the Civil Rights Act of 1957 established the U.S. **Commission** on Civil Rights. The commission helped enforce voter registration and school integration in the South during the coming years. It is also credited with helping change public opinion on civil rights among white Americans, making them more sympathetic to problems Black citizens often faced.

The bill also created a civil rights division within the U.S. Department of Justice. This meant that a special unit of the government was given the authority to bring cases on civil rights to court.

African American men and women registering to vote after the passage of the Civil Rights Act of 1957.

As Executive Director of the NAACP for more than twenty years, Roy Wilkins helped register thousands of African American voters in the 1950s and 1960s.

These additions in the bill acknowledged that civil rights issues needed to be addressed and that the federal government was willing to help. Yet voter protection, particularly for Black southerners, was still not as strong as it needed to be, and Roy Wilkins called it "a small crumb from Congress." It would take time and the tireless work of many Black and white supporters to bring about true change.

Nat King Cole (right), shown here with band members on his TV show, performed at the 1956 Republican National Convention in support of President Eisenhower.

The Nat King Cole Show

On November 5, 1956, singer Nat King Cole became the first Black American man to host a national TV program. At that time, Cole was one of the most popular stars in the country. The show was broadcast weekly on NBC, lasting 15 minutes and mostly featuring musical numbers. Many famous singers of diverse backgrounds appeared on the show such as Sammy Davis, Jr., Harry Belafonte, and Ella Fitzgerald. Cole also hosted white entertainers like Peggy Lee.

Ratings were high, but the show had a hard time finding a national sponsor. Corporations and advertisers were wary of backing a show with a Black host. Without financial supporters, the show couldn't last. The final episode appeared on December 17, 1957.

Segregation Still Strong

Passage of the Civil Rights Act of 1957 was a symbolic step in the right direction, but Black Americans did not notice an immediate change. On October 10, just one month after the bill was passed, Komla Gbedemah, a finance minister from the new nation of Ghana, and his secretary were denied service at a restaurant in Delaware. Dressed in business suits, the men pulled up to a Howard Johnson's restaurant. The server told them they could not sit inside the restaurant because "colored people are not allowed to eat in here." President Eisenhower, embarrassed by the incident, issued an official apology. Officials from Howard Johnson's told the Delaware restaurant manager that he must serve "anybody who comes to our doors." ■

Black schoolchildren stare through the fence of a playground for white children.

Little Rock's Central High School is now a National Historic Site.

The Legacy of 1957 in Civil Rights History

In 1957, progress moved slowly forward for civil rights. Although sometimes violent and full of hostility, the country had begun to awaken. Leaders stepped forward to create real change. The bravery of students like the Little Rock Nine forced politicians to follow through on promises. But resistance to integration was strong, and racism lived on in many parts of the country.

Black families ignore protesters as they enter a public school in Nashville, Tennessee.

The year 1957 marked a turning point in the career of Martin Luther King, Jr.

Martin Luther King, Jr., who still had not reached his 30th birthday, rose to prominence that year. His ability to inspire audiences and organize leaders became one of the primary influencers of change. In a letter to President Eisenhower after the Little Rock Nine had finally attended their first day of classes, King praised his actions: "I wish to express my sincere support for the stand you have taken to restore law and order in Little Rock, Arkansas . . . You should know that the overwhelming majority of southerners, Negro and white, stand firmly behind your resolute action."

Despite the progress made that year, the success of the Civil Rights Act of 1957 wasn't enough in the overall battle for civil rights. Opposition from southern politicians still prevented real change from happening. King remained optimistic that positive change was still to come and that activists for civil rights were on the right path, but their work was far from finished. ■

President Eisenhower issued Executive Order 10730 on September 23, 1957, giving troops from the 101st Airborne Division authority over the Arkansas National Guard.

Thurgood Marshall

The civil rights movement produced many leaders and activists who inspired the nation in its quest for tolerance and equality.

One of them was lawyer Thurgood Marshall. He is well known as one of the most successful lawyers of the 20th century. He first gained fame representing the **plaintiffs** in *Brown v. Board of Education*.

Marshall was born in 1908 in Baltimore, Maryland, where his father worked for the railroad and his mother was a teacher. Marshall grew up with an appreciation

Thurgood Marshall (left, standing) defends his client Donald Gaines Murray (center), who was denied entry into the University of Maryland Law School in 1935 due to race.

for the Constitution, and his father taught him how to debate. After graduation from high school, he attended Lincoln University. Kwame Nkrumah, the future prime minister of Ghana, was also a student at Lincoln while Marshall was there. After graduating, Marshall studied law at another all-Black school, Howard University.

Marshall believed that the only way for Black Americans to succeed was to receive an education, but white citizens and Black citizens did not have the same access to a quality education. He made it his mission to end segregation

After winning *Brown v. Board of Education*, Marshall helped student Autherine Lucy gain admission into the University of Alabama.

in schools. In 1934, he began working for the Baltimore branch of the NAACP, and over the next two decades, he won many cases involving racism. In 1957, three years after his success with the 1954 landmark case *Brown v. Board of Education*, Marshall and other lawyers from the NAACP successfully challenged Governor Orval Faubus's refusal to integrate Little Rock Central High School.

"History teaches that grave threats to liberty often come in times of urgency, when constitutional rights seem too extravagant to endure."

—THURGOOD MARSHALL

In 1961, newly elected President John F. Kennedy appointed Marshall as a judge to the U.S. Second Circuit Court of Appeals. Marshall made more than 100 decisions in four years, none of which were overturned by the Supreme Court. In 1965, President Lyndon Johnson appointed Marshall as the U.S. solicitor general, the first Black person to hold that position. In this role, he represented the federal government in arguments before the Supreme Court. In two years, he won 14 of the 19 cases he argued.

In 1967, Johnson appointed Marshall to the U.S. Supreme Court, the first African American to sit on the nation's highest court. In his new role, he supported rulings that protected individual rights and civil liberties. He helped decide important cases that would affect Americans for decades to come.

Accompanied by his family, Marshall is sworn in as the first African American Supreme Court justice.

For the next 24 years, Marshall served on the Court. In 1991 he retired because of failing health. That year, the second Black justice, Clarence Thomas, was appointed to the Court by President George H. W. Bush. Marshall died in 1993. He was buried in Arlington National Cemetery. Statues in courthouses and federal buildings mark his impact. Across America, numerous universities, airports, and schools have renamed buildings to honor the historic contributions of Justice Thurgood Marshall.

TIMELINE

The Year in Civil Rights

1957

Ghana becomes an independent nation.

MAY 17

The Prayer Pilgrimage in Washington, DC, gathers 25,000 people on the steps of the Lincoln Memorial.

JANUARY 10 & 11

Civil rights leaders gather in Atlanta, Georgia, to create the Southern Negro Leaders Conference on Transportation and Nonviolent Integration.

JUNE 13

Martin Luther King, Jr., is invited to the White House for the first time.

FEBRUARY 15

Another meeting, in New Orleans, Louisiana, of the Southern Negro Leaders Conference on Transportation and Nonviolent Integration was held to plan for the year ahead.

JULY 7

Althea Gibson becomes the first Black tennis player to win Wimbledon.

AUGUST

The Southern Christian Leadership Conference establishes headquarters in Atlanta.

SEPTEMBER 25

The Little Rock Nine attend their first day of school at Central High.

SEPTEMBER 4

The Little Rock Nine are blocked by National Guard troops from entering Little Rock Central High School.

OCTOBER 10

President Eisenhower apologizes to the new finance minister of Ghana, Komla Gbedemah, who was refused service at a restaurant in Delaware.

SEPTEMBER 9

The Civil Rights Act of 1957 is signed into law by President Dwight D. Eisenhower.

DECEMBER 17

The last episode of *The Nat King Cole Show* airs on television.

GLOSSARY

abolitionist (ab-uh-LISH-uh-nist) someone who worked to abolish slavery before the Civil War

activist (AK-tiv-ist) a person who works to bring about political or social change

boycott (BOI-kaht) a refusal to buy something or do business with someone as a protest

civilian (suh-VIL-yuhn) a person who is not a member of the armed forces or police force

civil liberties (SIV-uhl LIB-er-tees) freedom from governmental interference, especially the rights guaranteed by the Bill of Rights, such as free speech

civil rights (SIV-uhl rites) the individual rights that all members of a democratic society have to freedom and equal treatment under the law

commission (kuh-MISH-uhn) a group of people who meet to solve a particular problem or do certain tasks

desegregate (dee-SEG-ruh-gayt) to do away with the practice of separating people of different races in schools, restaurants, and other public places

discrimination (dis-krim-uh-NAY-shuhn) prejudice or unfair behavior to others based on differences in such things as race, gender, or age

effigy (EF-i-jee) a sculpture or model of a person

executive order (egg-ZEK-yuh-tiv OR-dur) an order having the force of law issued by the president of the United States

expel (ek-SPEL) to force someone to leave a school or organization

federal (FED-ur-uhl) national government, as opposed to state or local government

filibuster (FIL-uh-buhs-ter) an action such as a prolonged speech that obstructs progress in a legislative assembly while not technically prohibiting the required procedures

harass (huh-RAS) to bother or annoy someone again and again

infringe (IN-fring) to violate the rights of others

injunction (in-JUNK-shun) a court order requiring a person to do or stop doing a specific action

integrate (IN-tuh-grate) to include people of all races

Jim Crow (jim kro) the former practice of segregating Black people in the U.S.

literacy (LIT-ur-uh-see) the ability to read and write

lynching (LIN-ching) a sometimes public murder by a group of people, often involving hanging

nullify (NUHL-uh-fye) to make of no value or consequence

oppression (uh-PRESH-uhn) the act of treating people in a cruel and unjust way

plaintiff (PLAYN-tif) a person who brings a legal action

plight (plite) a dangerous, difficult, or unfortunate situation

poll tax (pohl taks) a tax of a fixed amount per person placed on adults and often linked to the right to vote

retribution (re-truh-BYOO-shuhn) the dispensing of punishment

righteousness (RYE-chuhs-ness) morally good

segregation (seg-ruh-GAY-shuhn) the act or practice of keeping people or groups apart

suffrage (SUHF-rij) the right to vote

telegram (TEL-uh-gram) a message that is sent by a system that uses a code of electrical signals sent by wire or radio

BIBLIOGRAPHY

Aretha, David. *The Story of the Little Rock Nine and School Desegregation in Photographs.* Enslow, 2014.

Belafonte, Harry. *We Are the Change: Words of Inspiration from Civil Rights Leaders.* Chronicle Books, 2019.

Kemp, Kristen. *Amazing Americans: Thurgood Marshall.* Teacher Created Materials, 2014.

"Southern Christian Leadership Conference." *National Park Service: Civil Rights,* September 10, 2013, https://www.nps .gov/subjects/civilrights/sclc.htm.

Troops from the 101st Airborne Division escort the Little Rock Nine as they enter Central High School on September 25, 1957.

https://blogs.loc.gov/teachers/2019/08/the-1957-march-on-washington-a-pilgrimage-for-rights-and-the-ballot/

eisenhowerlibrary.gov/research/online-documents/civil-rights-act-1957

history.com/this-day-in-history/central-high-school-integrated

history.house.gov/Historical-Highlights/1951-2000/the-civil-rights-act-of-1957/

kinginstitute.stanford.edu/encyclopedia/southern-christian-leadership-conference-sclc

kinginstitute.stanford.edu/king-papers/documents/statement-meeting-richard-m-nixon

nps.gov/chsc/learn/historyculture/timeline.htm

https://www.politico.com/story/2018/10/10/eisenhower-apologizes-racial-insult-1957-880971

INDEX

About the Author

Susan Taylor has contributed to articles for the History Channel, *Popular Science*, Scholastic, *National Geographic*, and more. Her publications cover biographies, history, science, and educational books. She also works for the YMCA in Estes Park, Colorado, as program director. When she's not writing, she enjoys hiking and spending time with her two kids.

PHOTO CREDITS